Andrea E. Davis has been in the field of crisis management since 1999, starting in the non-profit sector by developing Y2K crisis response plans. Andrea went on to serve in the city and county of San Francisco and in the US Federal Government as the emergency manager for the 12th District Federal Reserve Bank and as the external affairs director for the Federal Emergency Management Agency's Louisiana Recovery Office for Hurricane Katrina. While at FEMA, Andrea oversaw all media, intergovernmental and congressional activities for one of the U.S.' largest disaster recovery efforts, with a total recovery portfolio of over $25 billion.

For the past ten years, Andrea has led global, enterprise-wide crisis management departments for multi-national, Fortune 500 companies, the Walt Disney Company and the Walmart Corporation. Currently, she is the President and CEO of an SBA-certified, woman-owned, crisis management consulting firm, The Resiliency Initiative.

Andrea's passion is volunteer service which led to her selection as the Inaugural Emergency Manager of the Year by the International Association of Emergency Managers in 2018 and her induction into the Women's Hall of Fame for Emergency Management in 2013.

To my loving husband, thank you for always believing in my "crazy Andrea" ideas.

Andrea E. Davis

# I ONLY REMEMBER GRIEVANCES AND DESSERTS

What I Have Learned from the Cretins, Douchebags, and Vipers So Far

AUSTIN MACAULEY PUBLISHERS™
LONDON • CAMBRIDGE • NEW YORK • SHARJAH

**Copyright © Andrea E. Davis 2023**

All rights reserved. No part of this publication may be reproduced, distributed, or transmitted in any form or by any means, including photocopying, recording, or other electronic or mechanical methods, without the prior written permission of the publisher, except in the case of brief quotations embodied in critical reviews and certain other non-commercial uses permitted by copyright law. For permission requests, write to the publisher.

Any person who commits any unauthorized act in relation to this publication may be liable to criminal prosecution and civil claims for damages. This is a work of non-fiction; all stories in this are true.

**Ordering Information**
Quantity sales: Special discounts are available on quantity purchases by corporations, associations, and others. For details, contact the publisher at the address below.

**Publisher's Cataloguing-in-Publication data**
Davis, Andrea E.
I Only Remember Grievances and Desserts

ISBN 9798886930849 (Paperback)
ISBN 9798886930863 (Hardback)
ISBN 9781647501181 (ePub e-book)
ISBN 9798886930870 (Audiobook)

Library of Congress Control Number: 2023907207

www.austinmacauley.com/us

First Published 2023
Austin Macauley Publishers LLC
40 Wall Street, 33rd Floor, Suite 3302
New York, NY 10005
USA

mail-usa@austinmacauley.com
+1 (646) 5125767

# Table of Contents

| | |
|---|---|
| Introduction | 9 |
| Prelude: The "Path Less Traveled" Is Paved with Judgment and Spite So Best Make Truffles | 10 |
| "And That Has Made All the Difference" Chocolate Truffles | 13 |
| Worksheet Personal Assessment Roadmap | 15 |
| Case Study #1: The Cretin | 18 |
| Pity Party Bourbon Bread Pudding | 23 |
| Case Study #2: The Quintessential Douchebag | 25 |
| Didn't Your Mama Tell You? Never Piss Off a Redhead Cinnamon Buns | 30 |
| Reference Guide The Misogyny Matrix™ | 33 |
| Case Study #3: "The Special Place in Hell" Vipers | 36 |
| Killer Karma Carmel Chocolate Cupcakes | 41 |
| The BFF Viper | 43 |
| Older Andrea Insert | 52 |

| | |
|---|---|
| Kiss My A** Widely Inappropriate Drunken Black Forest Cake | 54 |
| Be a Mentor Hold the Door Open | 57 |
| Your Core Principles | 60 |
| Your Monthly Mantra | 62 |
| The Mentors | 63 |
| Ms. Avagene's Grace and Style Southern Tea Cakes | 68 |
| The Unflappable Mr. Threat | 69 |
| Mr. Threat's Calm, Cool, and | 75 |
| Collected Take-No-Crap Peach Cobbler | 75 |
| Dr. Jones | 77 |
| Dr. Jones's Self-Confident, Own Who You Are Hot Fudge Brownie Sundae | 80 |
| Rednado Goes into The Great Unknown | 82 |
| Rednado's Broken-Hearted Frozen Lemon Tart | 85 |
| Self-Acceptance Cherry Pie Recipe | 86 |
| Self-Acceptance Cherry Pie | 89 |

# Introduction

For twenty-plus years, I have made a career in the field of emergency management. I have worked in the nonprofit, government, and private sectors—doing all kinds of jobs, ranging from public affairs, 24/7 operations and strategic planning to crisis training. I have noticed several similarities across the years, jobs, and sectors: there are distinct personality types you will meet that will cause you to question your competence and abilities, there are personality types that cause you to question humanity in general, and finally, there are the people you will meet that will forever change you and your life course.

This workbook provides you with case studies, best practices, and response tactics regarding the various personality types I have worked with through the years. My intent is to provide you with examples of how I dealt with each situation and give you tips and tools on how to handle similar situations and personality types. And if all else fails, I hope I would have provided you with some good recipes to help you think through your course of action before you respond.

# Prelude: The "Path Less Traveled" Is Paved with Judgment and Spite So Best Make Truffles

Thirty years ago, I decided to go down Robert Frost's proverbial "path less traveled." I graduated from high school eight months pregnant. Though some thought I was brave, most thought I was an abomination.

I had to fight with the administration to be able to walk with my classmates. Even though it was 1991, I was considered an embarrassment to the school. It was important to me to accept my diploma in person. I had worked hard for it. I was graduating with an over 3.5 GPA. I had represented my school at Girl's State and as a young Congressional Leader and won first place in the county literary festival and drama festival. I had earned this important passage of life just as much as my classmates, so what if I was pregnant?

Even though I had consciously decided I wasn't going to care what people thought of me, I was ill prepared for the visceral reaction I would receive from the graduation audience, as I walked to get my diploma. People spat on me and threw garbage at me. I was called every variation of the word "slut" that you can imagine (*harlot remains my favorite; it almost seems rather classy.*)

It took everything in my power to continue to hold my head high and accept my diploma. However, in my heart of hearts, all I truly wanted to do was run, run as far away as possible.

At my weakest and most vulnerable moment, I had experienced absolute cruelty because I made a choice that others didn't agree with, and they felt I flaunted it. I could feel the weight of their judgment. Without understanding or any sort of conversation, these perfect strangers felt justified to publicly assault me.

I know it is odd to say this, but I am thankful for that experience. It set in motion my drive to become an advocate for others, especially those who are marginalized or do not have a voice. My graduation experience taught me the value of compassion, a fundamental principle in my professional field of emergency management. I felt so alone and afraid. I decided that very moment, I never wanted anyone to ever feel that way; that terrible, painful moment in my history began my quest to help others feel safe and become resilient.

I am also thankful for that experience because at a young age, it forced me to find a way to deal with hurt and pain in a productive manner. Obviously, being eight months pregnant, I could not go out celebrating with my classmates. So I went home and decided I would start learning how to cook, and my love affair with baking began.

Creating desserts became my way of handling stressful and hurtful situations. As a graduation present, I was given a *Betty Crocker* cookbook. As I thumbed through the book, I admired how cooking, especially baking, had such attention to detail. Just a quarter cup of flour is the difference between a biscuit and a scone. I felt pretty beat up by my graduation experience, but I noticed that as I read the cookbook, my focus started to change, especially when I got to the dessert section.

The dessert became my manifestation of the situation, and with every ingredient I added, it helped me figure out an approach to handling whatever situation I was dealing with. Baking became my therapy and, through the years, has helped me work through many problems. As I could afford it, I began collecting cookbooks; second-hand ones were my favorite because you could almost smell the desserts of the past. Years later, I would discover French cooking through Julia Child and I received the Joy of Cooking as a gift, which opened a whole new world of different ways to cook and bake.

I still remember graduation night like it was yesterday, and I still remember what dessert I made that night to ease my pain. I needed the perfect pick-me-up. Something simple. A dessert that was equal parts process and creativity. The simple yet elegant chocolate truffle. To this day, I make truffles anytime I need a pick-me-up, and it serves as a reminder about how tough experiences can define who you are and help you determine what is most important to you.

# "And That Has Made All the Difference" Chocolate Truffles

*Excerpted from* the Betty Crocker Cookbook, *circa* 1990

### Ingredients

- 6 ounces semisweet baking chocolate or white chocolate baking bars, chopped
- 2 tablespoons butter
- cup heavy whipping cream
- 1 cup semisweet chocolate chips or white vanilla baking chips
- A splash of your favorite cordial—raspberry and orange are two of my favs!
- 1 tablespoon shortening
- Finely chopped nuts or candy decorations, if desired

### Directions

Line a cookie sheet with foil. In a 2-quart saucepan, melt the baking chocolate over low heat, stirring constantly; stir in butter until melted and smooth. Remove from heat; stir in whipping cream. Pour the mixture into a small bowl. Refrigerate for 10 to 15 minutes—stirring frequently, just until thick enough to hold a shape. Drop the mixture by rounded measuring teaspoonfuls onto a lined cookie sheet. Return to the refrigerator for 5 to 10 minutes or until firm enough to shape. Shape into balls. Freeze uncovered for 30 minutes. In a 1-quart saucepan, heat the chocolate chips and shortening over low heat, stirring constantly, until the chocolate has melted, and the mixture is smooth; remove from heat. Using two forks, dip and roll chocolate balls, one at a time, into the melted chocolate; tap off excess chocolate. Place on a lined cookie sheet. Immediately sprinkle with nuts. If the chocolate has cooled too much, reheat. Repeat with the remaining chocolate balls. Refrigerate the truffles for about 10 minutes, or until the chocolate is set. Store in a covered container in the refrigerator. Remove from the refrigerator, about 10 minutes before serving.

# Worksheet Personal Assessment Roadmap

In 2014, I was approached by several female colleagues asking if I would be their mentor. Being in a traditionally male-dominated profession, there were few women in leadership roles. I welcomed the opportunity to share what has worked for me through the years and develop a collective group of women who help each other think through challenging situations. I created a mentoring group called "The Future Women Leaders of Security" and developed the assessment below for each member of the group. Head to The Misogyny Matrix ™ to see how this was viewed by male leadership and colleagues.

## Fundamentals

- What is your brand (i.e., how you want to be perceived)?
- What are your personal stakes (i.e., what you believe in about who you are that is nonnegotiable)?
- Who is your hero and why?
- What are your professional objectives (next five years, ten years, etc.)?

**Accountability Roadmap**: How will you make your goals happen? How will you hold yourself accountable?

*Here is my sample roadmap as developed in 2014.*

Professional Goal: I would like to be FEMA's administrator when I leave Disney in ten years.

How do I see myself achieving my goal?

- Maintain relationships at a federal level. Join the National Advisory Council.
- Leverage existing relationship as vice-chair of the Red Cross.
- Be seen as a leader in private-sector partnerships. Host a kick-off conference in New Orleans, LA.
- Launch Los Angeles County's culture of preparedness campaign.

**Professional Goals:**

| Questions | Your Response |
|---|---|
| What is important to you? | |
| What is your defining life moment? | |
| What makes you smile? | |
| (how do you want to be perceived)? | |
| What are your personal stakes (what do you believe in; what about you is nonnegotiable)? | |
| Who is your hero and why? | |

| Objective | Start Date | Action Steps | Quarterly Check in Notes |
|---|---|---|---|
| | | | |
| | | | |
| | | | |
| | | | |
| | | | |

# Case Study #1 The Cretin

The Cretin—a.k.a. the mansplainer, misogynist, all-around horrible human being.

Ahhhhh, the Cretin. We all know him; he is at every workplace, worldwide. I have met him many times in my 20+ years, in emergency management. There is seriously no amount of mandatory HR/sensitivity training that will ever have an impact on his behavior. Cretins are typically large in stature, so they make you feel like you are a tiny, helpless mouse. They are always telling borderline offensive jokes, and if you even raise an eyebrow, you get a "What? Geez, a man can't say anything anymore without offending someone." The Cretin is smart enough to not say something overtly inappropriate, but the placement of their gaze, when saying "you look really nice today", immediately makes you feel dirty and tells you exactly what they are thinking. Any complement he gives you about your work is dripping with sarcasm and belittlement.

Here are a few phrases I have received from Cretins over the years:

- "Good job on that project. It must be nice to be given such an easy assignment."
- "Oh, you are really loud." (Oh, you haven't heard loud yet.)
- "Only a woman could get away with saying that."

- "Who takes care of your son while you work?"
- "Do you have Tourette's, because you keep repeating yourself". (no, idiot, you are not listening, so I am trying to repeat myself and speak slowly for you)
- "Unless you have been shot at, you really can't say that you have emergency management field experience."
- "You look yummy."
- "I don't want to hear about daycare issues. That's the whole reason women shouldn't work outside the home"
- "You are too pretty" or "Your boobs are too big to be taken seriously."

And of course, the classic

- "You are a bitch." (ALWAYS ask why they think you are a bitch. They will turn bright red, possibly attempt to hit you and just walk away. If they actually can come up with a "why," you will have a good laugh.)

The Cretin's behavior is so pervasive, so vile, compared to modern professional standards that when you are presented with it, you immediately think it must be a joke. Heck, it's not 1962, and it is reasonable for you to believe that people don't live under rocks!

I still have a vivid memory of the first time I met a Cretin. I was working for the federal government on an emergency response effort in the South. This larger-than-life man stood towering over me, yelling and going off at me, and saying something ridiculous, like he outranked me, and I better not question his authority. I remember, literally busting up, laughing, and saying out loud, "Oh, I just figured it out, you are a sexist! I haven't met one before." I can still see the flash of anger on his face as I walked away. (Note: I immediately ran into the women's restroom. I was truly terrified by him but didn't want him to see that. I saw his eyes. His death stars. This guy truly meant me harm—murder or worse).

It was with this same Cretin that I experienced one of my most embarrassing professional moments. In 2011, the US had one of its largest responses to Mississippi River flooding, and it marked only the third time in US history that all national spillways had been opened. I was deployed from FEMA's Katrina Recovery Office to support the region's effort in Baton Rouge, as the public affairs officer. I was the only female and the only nonregional employee deployed. It was made crystal clear to me I was NOT "one of them," and they didn't want me there. In fact, they made it clear every second of every day. They ensured there was no room for me at the lunchroom table, so I had to eat at my desk. They gave me wrong directions during dark and stormy nights in hopes I would get so lost and end up in a ditch (which one night I did). Now, mind you, these are grown ass men! Many with wives and daughters. Their behavior was not only unacceptable, it was deplorable. In addition to the dealing with continuous harassment, I was also dealing with a tough work situation. We were responding to a crisis which meant very long hours, with little sleep. It was not uncommon that I would be up at 5:00

a.m. then fielding calls from Washington, DC, until after midnight. About a week into the response, after I had been up for close to 30 hours, the Federal Coordinating Officer (FCO, basically the person in charge of the response effort) called a meeting with his direct reports. I headed into the room, and the Cretin physically blocked me from entering the room. At this point, my tolerance was gone. I had had enough of the harassment and finally found my voice.

Me: "Please move."

Cretin: "Make me."

I raised my voice and let the FCO know I was there, and he said I should come in. I just stared at the Cretin dead in the eye, smiled, and pushed past him.

I sat across from the FCO, and the Cretin sat right next to him—staring straight at me, seething with anger.

*(Remember, this guy was like 6 10", 1000 pounds. Of course, I am exaggerating, but that's how it felt. He was very scary)*

The FCO started going through the tasks of the day, and the Cretin jumped in after each sentence and started verbally attacking me:

- "You failed to make sure we knew about the press conference in a timely fashion."
- "You failed, again, by not setting up the call at 0500."

I remember just sitting there in shock. Why is the FCO not stopping him? Why is he allowing this to happen to me?

I started blinking profusely. Then… **I committed the worst sin a female can commit in the workplace… I started crying—not just a tear a two, but all out sobbing, snotty, snorty, hysterical sobbing.**

*Flip to "The Unflappable Mr. threat" for the continuation of this story. In the meantime, pour yourself a nice toll glass of bourbon while you make…*

# Pity Party Bourbon Bread Pudding

## Ingredients

- 1 loaf French bread, cut into cubes or if you are dealing with a real jerk, ripping the bread apart is VERY therapeutic!
- 4 cups milk
- 3 large eggs, beaten
- 1 cup sugar
- 1 cup light brown sugar
- 1/4 cup butter
- 2 tablespoons pure vanilla extract

Note: Most bread puddings include golden raisins. I despise raisins, so I never cook with them. But throw a 1/3 cup in if you like them!)

## Bourbon Sauce

- 1/2 cup butter softened
- 1 cup sugar
- 1 large egg, well beaten
- 2 tablespoons bourbon (I am old school, so I always lean toward the classic Jim Beam)

## Directions

Combine the bread and milk in a large mixing bowl; set aside for 5 minutes. Add eggs, sugar, butter, and vanilla; stir well. Spoon the mixture into a greased pan (a casserole dish is best, but any 2.5—3-quart pan will do). Bake, uncovered, at 325°F for 1 hour, or until firm. Cool in a pan for a good 30 minutes. While the pudding is cooling, make the bourbon sauce. Combine the butter and sugar in a small saucepan; apply low heat, stirring frequently until sugar dissolves. Add egg, stirring briskly with a wire whisk until well blended. Cook over medium heat for about 2 minutes or until the sauce is light yellow and smooth. Remove from heat and stir in bourbon.

Grab a good scope of the pudding, put it on your favorite plate, and drizzle on the bourbon sauce *(or lop on, depending on your mood!)*

# Case Study #2
# The Quintessential Douchebag

Here are common characteristics of the Douchebag:

- Always operates off rumor and gossip and even brings them up as fact in staff meetings
- Allows in fighting—in fact, thrives off it—because it takes away from you finding out how incompetent they are
- Loves to say, "What would you like me to do about it?" or "It has always been this way"
- Will repeatedly share personal stories specific about a loss or hardship to try to justify their inaction
- Are kings of circular reasoning and experts at gaslighting

Unfortunately, the Douche is hands down the worst boss you can ever have, because they will never stand up for you, support you, encourage you, or even give you an ounce of helpful advice. They will perpetually share stories from their perceived "glory days," and with a Douche, it will always be someone else's fault for not supporting you.

They are terrified of your ability, confidence, self-respect, you name it. They are terrified of you because they are spineless weasels. They are usually placed in positions of authority because they typically attach themselves to a Cretin or Queen Bee and leech off their spoils. They only know how to bend over and say yes to higher-ups.

By not taking a stand or supporting their staff, they don't cause waves and are generally perceived by upper leadership as very loyal.

They are the cockroaches of the working world, and sadly, there are a lot of them. They are everywhere, even when interviewing for a job.

In late 2018, I was flown out to make a pitch to create a new position for a nonprofit I dearly love and have volunteered for most of my life. I was so excited about this opportunity; this was going to be a good strategic professional move for me if it came to fruition. I had put together a one-pager of the position and my idea, and the recruiter had set up a day full of interviews, starting with all top leadership and ending with the head of HR. I remember the entire plane ride, walking through my talking points and the different areas I wanted to highlight. I cyberstalked all the individuals I was going to be interviewing with so I could make sure to bring up relevant examples to relate to them. It was hard to sleep because I was excited and nervous all at once, but I felt ready to go.

My interview was at 7 a.m., so I was dressed by 6 a.m. and walked over to the headquarters office.

The interview took place at various offices in a very historic building in Washington, DC. I have always wanted to work in DC, and the thought that I could potentially have an office that would be within walking distance of the Lincoln Memorial *(my favorite)* seemed like a dream. I remember anxiously awaiting to be called into a conference room for my first interview. It was a panel with three of the organization's top leaders (two men and one woman, all with very decorated careers in emergency management).

The door opened, and I was asked to come sit. I felt I was entering a room of greatness, and it was hard to contain my excitement. I was almost giddy. I took a big breath, slowly exhaled, smiled, and introduced myself to everyone. I handed out my one-pager and sat down. After the pleasantries, I went right into my pitch of why I thought creating my idea for a new position would be a smart investment for the organization. I got a lot of head nods and yeses. One of the men and the woman started asking some very probing questions, and we had a good dialogue. He then pulled out my resume and asked if my time with FEMA coincided with that of the other male leader in the room.

Before I could answer, the other male, who hadn't really said anything or particularly looked at me since I started, said, "We didn't have any crossover. I was at headquarters; she was just in a recovery office telling stories."

I was a bit stunned by the interjection but kept my cool and said, "I don't think we did have any interaction. My responsibilities were focused on external affairs specific to Hurricane Katrina recovery and I was based down in New Orleans. Telling the story of the recovery process was a big focus since it is still the largest US recovery effort." I thought I made a pretty nice pivot. However, the Douchebag kept coming after me.

"I read your position pitch, and you really think you have the experience to fill it?"

I turned to face him directly and replied, "Yes." I listed the various ways I felt I was qualified for it.

Looking straight at me, he said, "I totally disagree. You have never run something of the stature you are recommending."

The other male jumped in and said, "You currently lead the entire global crisis management function for the Walt Disney Company, don't you?"

Trying to get my confidence back, I nodded and said, "Yes."

It took me a minute, but I was able to get my composure back and started showcasing examples of what I had done or was currently doing that actually gave me the idea to pitch this position, and why I felt it was a natural next step for me.

The Douchebag shook his head and said, "I have done this type of work for fifty years. I have worked with exceptional individuals. You, young lady, do not have what it takes." He stood up and walked out of the conference room.

I had no idea what to do.

The female just stared at the table, shuffling papers. The other male looked at me and said, "We really appreciate you taking the time to fly out here from California. It was nice meeting you."

I got up and thanked them and walked out of the conference room. I went to the front reception area having no clue what to do. My next interview wasn't for several hours, and it was obvious it didn't matter if I interviewed well or not. I wasn't going to get the support I needed for the position, let alone get selected to fill it.

I was crestfallen. I asked myself, do I just leave and get an earlier flight home? I decided to stay. I reminded myself this was an organization that I loved and had supported my whole life. An organization I feel I owe my career to. I was not going to let one Douchebag take that from me. I knew I had a good idea. So what if the timing is off? He is bound to retire one day, and I will make the pitch again. OR his boss will retire, and I will interview for the job and get it... then we will see who has what it takes.

This Douchebag instilled in me the power of focus, patience, and polite directness. I did not accept anything that man said to me that day, but I wasn't going to allow his inferiority complex to degrade my professionalism. Who would it have served if I stormed out the room or left the interview process early? If I had done either of those two things, I would have played into his narrative about me. From that day forward, I started a "Stress Mantra": Inhale focus, exhale toxic words. Repeat... and make yourself some Never Piss Off a Redhead Cinnamon Buns!

Actually, learning to bake anything that uses yeast will set you up for success in many areas of your life. If you don't throw the bowl of deflated mush after your first few tries of trying to bake something with yeast, you have learned the true meaning of patience!

# Didn't Your Mama Tell You? Never Piss Off a Redhead Cinnamon Buns

**Ingredients**

**Rolls**

- 1/2 cup unsalted butter
- 1 cup milk
- 2 packages regular or fast-acting dry yeast
- 1/3 cup granulated sugar
- 1 teaspoon salt
- 3 ½ 4 cups all-purpose flour
- 1 large egg
- Cooking spray

**Filling**

- 1/2 cup brown sugar
- 2 teaspoons ground cinnamon
- 1/4 cup butter room temperature

## Glaze

- 1 cup powdered sugar
- 1 tablespoon butter or margarine, room temperature
- 1/2 teaspoon vanilla
- 1—2 tablespoons heavy whipping cream

## Directions

**Rolls**: Melt the butter in a small saucepan; stir in milk. Remove from the stovetop and whisk in yeast until foamy. In a bowl, combine sugar, salt, 3 cups flour, yeast mixture, and the egg. Stir until nice and moist. Add additional flour to firm up the dough. Knead the dough in the bowl for around 8 minutes, only adding more flour if the dough seems too sticky. Shape the dough into a ball. Grab a paper towel, wipe the small saucepan, and spread the leftover butter and sugar around a large bowl. Place the dough in the bowl. Cover the dough with plastic wrap and let it rise in a warm place for about 2 hours or until it doubles in size. Spray a large baking dish with cooking spray. When the dough has doubled in size, sprinkle the remaining flour on a large cutting board; lay it and roll the dough out a good foot and half. Make the filling.

Filling: Mix the butter, brown sugar, cinnamon, and salt. Sprinkle the filling all over the dough (don't forget the edges!). Roll the dough like you are rolling up a carpet. Cut into six to eight pieces. Place the pieces in the prepared baking dish, cover with plastic wrap, and let them rise for another hour and half. Preheat the oven to 350° F. Bake the rolls for 25-30 minutes. They should be a nice golden brown.

Glaze: Mix all ingredients together. If it's a bit lumpy, grab a hand mixer and mix until nice and smooth. After the rolls cool for about 10 minutes, drizzle on the glaze. Voila!

Before I move onto the deplorable women you will meet in the workplace, I would like to provide you with a reference guide that has helped me navigate the Cretins and Douchebags through the years – The Misogyny Matrix ™

$$\frac{\textbf{Platitudes + Placing}}{\textbf{Patronizing}} = \textbf{Misogyny}$$

# Reference Guide
# The Misogyny Matrix™

**Beware of the Three Ps:**

$$\frac{\text{Platitudes + Placating}}{\text{Patronizing}} = \text{Misogyny}$$

Women, be on heightened alert if you hear any of the following phrases in the workplace. All statements below were said straight to my face, during work hours:

- "You are the best emergency manager I have ever worked with, but you are too… [insert any sexist comment you want: difficult, emotional, aggressive, loud]."
- In a staff meeting, a colleague said, "Someone really needs to put you in your place."
- An HR director opined, "You are best served to taper your passions."
- *(Referenced in the Personal Assessment Worksheet section)* When I started a women's mentorship group, my male executive leadership coined it the "Subversive Women's Club." (My response? I made us all beauty queen sashes that said *Subversive Women's Club* in bright red that we wore to every meeting!)

- After looking me up and down, "You are Andrea Davis? Um, I wonder how you moved up through the ranks so quickly."
- "We have ways of working here. Never talk directly to anyone in the field; you must go through me first."

## So How Do You Counteract The Misogyny Matrix ™? With Professional Jujitsu!

- People will always express their doubts about you either verbally or through facial expressions (e.g., eye-rolling) because it is easier to be critical than supportive. Smile and make eye contact with them. Say "hmm" or "OK."
- Never accept bad behavior. Politely call someone out and don't apologize because they are uncomfortable with you not tolerating it.
- When dealing with a bully conversationalist, say "I haven't spoken in the past five minutes. I am going to jump in now."
- When dealing with someone who stole or took credit for your work. Via email or publicly, say "Thank you so much for highlighting my work. I would like to appreciate the team that supported it… [list names]."
- Don't underestimate the incredible power of not saying anything and taking copious notes. Silence can be deafening, especially to Douchebags and Cretins.

- If you are in a meeting, whether in person or virtually, and people are being abusive to you, get up and walk out. You will be asked what you are doing. Say, "You are being disrespectful and wasting everyone's time. When you are ready to have a productive meeting, I will return." (Yes, I realize this takes a degree of moxie, and I have only done this twice in my career, both when I was in a position of authority. But seriously, life is way too short to put up with abusive behavior. People will only change if you call them out.)
- Pay it forward, weaponize your pain and anger. Write down your experiences, so I can learn from you!

# Case Study #3 "The Special Place in Hell" Vipers

Writing about the workplace Vipers is depressing. I agree wholeheartedly with Eleanor Roosevelt when she said, "There is a special place in hell for women who do not support each other." I really thought once we all got out of high school, the "mean girl" would be gone, and we would all support and encourage each other.

Unfortunately, I found the workplace just the opposite of that, and mean girls, sadly, still exist. In fact, I have had a tougher time dealing with females in the workplace than I have males. That is probably due, in part, to my expectation. I was fully aware that trying to work my way through the ranks in a male-dominated field, I would be in for a daily dose of harassment and misogyny; however, I wasn't prepared to deal with the Vipers.

Regardless of your workplace or field, you need to prepare yourself for all types of people. I recommend assuming the best out of folks and presume good intent, but do not be blind to human nature, weakness, and just plain bad apples.

### The Queen Bee

Typical species: Older female with weight issues who has had to "deal with a lot" through the years and "you just don't know how bad it was." You owe them everything for all their years of trailblazing and suffering.

A Queen Bee is nothing more than a bully. They are insecure and green with envy with your accomplishments, your looks, everything about you. If you present yourself with your sense of style and confidence and stand by your work, they will come after you. They will be very overt about trying to belittle you and tear you down.

Here is a list of phrases Queen Bee Vipers have said to my face through the years:

- "You are a power-hungry bitch." This person literally, and I wish I were joking, spit on me IN THE OFFICE.
- "Boy, I'm not sure you will be taken seriously with your boobs being so big."
- "Gosh, those pearls look almost real."
- "I am not sure your dress meets with the dress code." (Ask for the company dress code; 99% of the time one doesn't exist. you should not be surprised when you find out there isn't one)
- "You are just not management material, so I wouldn't apply for the job opening." (Usually, this is code for they are applying for that job or did and got rejected. APPLY FOR THE JOB! Your confidence will drive a Queen Bee insane.)
- "This is by far the stupidest thing I have seen [heard of, etc.]." This will be regarding a new idea you have. (Pitch your idea to the "big boss." trust me, they will love it.)

- After I presented on live TV, a Queen Bee said, "Here is list of mistakes I found in the information you just shared. Sorry I didn't catch them before I gave you the talking points."

So how do you deal with a Queen Bee? Just the same as you would a bully. You stand your ground and ignore them. Be prepared; this will cause them to come after you. Queen Bees live in a "dog eat dog" world, and the two of you cannot coexist in their reality. Remember, the Queen Bee is so insecure she is blinded by her fear that people will see through her and find out she is nothing.

Ignoring a Queen Bee will infuriate them. They will try to smear you by gossiping and spreading lies. Unfortunately, my last dealing with a Queen Bee came at a time when a Douchebag was my manager, and Douchebags make the worst managers. He would even bring up the rumors he had heard from the Queen Bee in our team staff meetings!

This was appalling on many levels. I not only had to defend myself against a bully and her lies but also had a manager who didn't have my back. I know it will be hard, but you must stand up for yourself. If you wait for someone to stand up for you or even stand by you, it may never come, and your reputation can get destroyed in the process.

Furthermore, never allow any rumor or gossip to go unaddressed. You must have zero tolerance for them. A direct, while looking the offender in the eye, "This is simply not true. Please stop spreading lies about me" will get the Queen Bee to shut down 90 percent of the time. However, I have witnessed Queen Bees double down and get even more hostile and more defensive. One Queen Bee repeat offender aggressively charged at me and became violent—she threw a book at me (in a staff meeting!) and spat on me while calling me a power-hungry bitch. Seriously, the workplace should never look like an episode of *Game of Thrones!*

In these extreme incidents, you must document, tell your boss, and then tell HR. However, do not get your hopes up that there will be any sort of consequences rendered on the Queen Bee offender. In the example I shared above, I did everything right. I told my boss immediately after it occurred. I didn't even get an "I am sorry that happened" from him. I got "Your predecessor thought she was a bully as well." So she was a known problem and was not being handled? I then went to HR, got a "Thanks for reporting your concern to us," and never heard back from them. To my knowledge, there never were any consequences for the bullying behavior, and she was even promoted.

When you take a stand against bad or wrong behavior, it is difficult to stomach when you are not supported or there is no change or consequences rendered. You might even be made to feel like you are too sensitive or even gaslighted. This example of Queen Bee behavior was witnessed by several individuals, many in leadership positions *(all of whom had a* duty *and obligation* to *report* to *HR).* These individuals were just as culpable for perpetuating a hostile environment.

Try to step back and acknowledge what's going on; if something is wrong, it's wrong. Never accept that it isokayto be bullied, disrespected, or rumored about. If you ever witness a Queen Bee in action, no matter your level, you must stand up against it. Just because you might not get the public flogging you expect to be rendered on the Queen Bee, that doesn't mean Karma will not catch up with them. Plus, you don't know how many folks you might help down the road because you documented their behavior.

Now, treat yourself for being brave and go make yourself some Killer Karma Carmel Chocolate Cupcakes!

# Killer Karma Carmel Chocolate Cupcakes

Ingredients

Cupcakes

- 1 cup all-purpose flour
- 1/2 cup cocoa (Ghirardelli is my favorite!)
- 1/2 teaspoon baking powder
- 1/2 teaspoon baking soda
- 1/4 teaspoon salt
- 1/2 cup unsalted butter, melted
- 1 cup dark brown sugar
- 2 eggs
- 2 teaspoons vanilla extract
- 3/4 cup buttermilk

Chocolate Buttercream

- 1 1/2 cup unsalted butter, softened
- 1/2 cup cocoa
- 1/2 cup melted dark chocolate chips (same as the cocoa, Ghirardelli is the best)
- 5 cups confectioner's sugar
- 1/2 cup heavy whipping cream

- 2 teaspoons vanilla extract

## Directions

Cupcakes: Preheat the oven to 350° F, and line a muffin tin with cupcake cups. In a large bowl, sift together the flour, cocoa, baking soda, baking powder, and salt. In a separate bowl, mix together the melted butter and brown sugar until smooth. Add the eggs one at a time. Add the vanilla and mix well. Add half of the flour mixture to the butter and sugar mixture. Stir gently until just combined. Add half the buttermilk and mix. Add the rest of the flour and buttermilk; stir gently. Don't *overmix; the cupcakes could turn into hockey pucks if you do!* Fill the muffin cups about ¾ full. Bake in the oven for approximately 18—20 minutes. When a toothpick is inserted and comes out clean, your cupcakes are done. Cool in the tin for about five minutes, then place on a wire rack.

Chocolate Buttercream: Mix all ingredients until lightened and fluffy. If the frosting seems a bit too thick, add a teaspoon or two of water.

After the cupcakes have cooled for about an hour, frost them with the buttercream. If you are feeling especially down, sprinkle on some of the leftover chocolate chips!

# The BFF Viper

By far, the worst creature I have come across in my professional career is the BFF Viper. You see a Queen Bee coming a mile away, but the BFF Viper you sometimes never see coming. Sadly, I have come across many BFF Vipers in my career, and each time I encountered them, I was completely blindsided by their betrayal. This person is way more than a colleague; you truly believe they are your best friend. You socialize, know intimate details about each other's lives, and commiserate about work issues. By all practical purposes, they are your friend.

However, what you don't know is that the BFF Viper is secretly plotting against you, waiting to betray you when you trust them the most. They are seething with insecurity and envious of your confidence, strength, and mostly, your ability to see opportunities instead of hurdles. You watch their dog when they go on vacation, help them finalize a large project, or even write a promotion justification for them. As you believe your friendship is deepening, the BFF Viper is recoiling inside and waiting for the moment to strike and take you down. The nicer you are, the more they are trying to gain leverage on you. They believe you are a threat to their upward mobility, raise, bonus, and so forth. As you trust them explicitly, they are plotting and even starting rumors about you. They start talking about you behind your back, rolling their eyes when you speak in a meeting, even sending emails taking credit for what you have done. Even if you get wind of their behavior, you do not believe it. They are your best work friend. You are inseparable. You mentor and encourage each other. Why would you ever expect them to have been plotting against you since day one? However, fear and insecurity are powerful drivers, and I have seen them make people do terrible things.

Early in my career, I was betrayed in the worst way by a BFF Viper. This betrayal was significant because I truly believed the BFF Viper was a dear friend; she had been my mentor for years. I continuously sought her guidance, I trusted her. She seemed to be a true friend UNTIL I was promoted to her rank, a rank she had been at for over 10 years, and I was being promoted in just a little over three years.

To me, my promotion meant I got to work with my work BFF more often. I was excited, so when my boss wanted to do a team restructure and asked if I had any problem reporting to my best friend, I, of course, said no. Little did I know that my BFF had gone to my boss saying she was concerned that I was too green for the promotion and that I might need some direct oversight. Almost immediately, my new boss/BFF started giving me out-of-scope projects, such as putting together the department budget, or administrative tasks, such as tracking team trainings. Even though these extra projects were causing me to stay late and get in early, I jumped at the chance to learn new things. However, this was a significant personal hardship for me because I had a 90-mile one-way work commute; with traffic, this was usually around three hours each way. I would try to take a bus in, but then there were nights I had to stay late and missed the bus, causing me to stay the night with friends. I would end up missing countless dinners with my family, my son's football games, helping my son with homework, and so on. I kept telling myself, it is just a learning curve. My friend needs help; it's just a tough moment in time. I knew she was giving me these projects to help my professional growth, right?

WRONG! This was designed to tear down my confidence. She was anticipating I would fail or would come to her saying that I needed to scale back because of my personal situation. When that didn't occur, she just started layering on more and more work—such as organizing the department-wide fundraiser, which meant more time away from my family. (Note: my job title at the time was emergency manager) I continued to cheerfully say, "No problem, I will make it work." I seriously had no idea that this woman that I had looked up to for years and considered my mentor and my best friend was secretly plotting against me, trying to take me down. The red flags were always there but I was just too naive to see them. Because of my fast projection, even receiving the organization's "rising star" award, she was seething with jealousy. She had never been promoted in her tenure with the organization, and she couldn't stand the "unfairness" of me getting all the attention. She was going to enact her revenge, and it was going to be against me.

Putting together a department-wide budget is daunting, especially for someone who has no background in finance or any training. However, I knew if I could understand the process and have a general understanding of financial principles, it would serve my career well, so even though it wasn't part of my job description and I knew I had a learning curve, I was excited about the opportunity when my BFF gave the task to me. (Note: she had done the department budget for nearly five years and is an accountant.) It didn't occur to me that anything was up when my BFF would leave the office at 5:30 p.m. and I would stay until midnight pulling everything together. It didn't even bother me when she arrived at work at 10 a.m. and I got there at 7 a.m. and she would say "Had to take the kid to school" while I hadn't seen my son in two days. I truly believed she gave me this opportunity for my professional growth.

On the last night of the budget season, I got everything wrapped up and submitted. I remember proudlywalking out of the office at around 11 p.m. I was really proud of the work I had done.

The following day, the head of operations came over to my director and my BFF and let them know he was very impressed with the budget package I had put together: "One of the best I have ever seen." My director told me how proud he was of me. I was beaming with pride and was so happy I made my department look good. I had no idea my BFF was boiling with jealousy and anger inside.

Two days later, my BFF came into my office and closed the door behind me—stating, with a stern tone, "We need to talk." She sat down and said, "Several teammates have come to me in private, stating that you make them uncomfortable with how you dress." I remember just staring at her blankly. This was so random, so out of the blue. She proceeded to say, "It is my job as your boss to take this seriously and investigate this." *(No, it isn't. If these were real complaints, most organizations require a manager to bring the situation to human resources. It is HR's responsibility to investigate accusations of a hostile or sexual harassment nature)*

I was literally in shock. I couldn't stop blinking and staring at her. I was speechless.

BFF Viper: "Do you have anything to say for yourself?"

I finally got the courage to find words as tears started rolling down my face.

Me: "You are my friend. I don't understand. I wear a business suit every day. You know I don't dress inappropriately. How could you even entertain this?"

BFF Viper: "I am not your friend. I am your boss, and I need to take complaints about my staff seriously." (Still *no* mention of HR)

Me: (Still blinking, trying to stop the tears) "OK, I would like to meet with you and our director. This doesn't make any sense to me. I feel like my reputation is being unfoundedly attacked."

BFF Viper: "Fine. I will set something up." She turned and left my office.

I sat there stunned and started bawling. I had no idea what had just happened to me. For the past six months, I had worked so hard with great personal expense. I was exhausted from literally working 15-hour days and pretty much abandoning my husband and teenage son. Her words just kept running through my head: I make people uncomfortable with how I dress. I looked down at what I was wearing that day—a three-piece pant suit and a turtleneck top. I don't know how I could have been inappropriate, and in my many years with the organization, no one ever said anything about how I dressed other than compliments I remember walking to the bus station almost in a trance, and as soon as I got on the bus, I cried for nearly the full three straight hours home.

I felt humiliated and, most of all, betrayed by my best friend.

Our director was out of town for a week, so the next few days were some of the most uncomfortable and excruciating of my life. I had to walk past her office to get to mine, so every time I would walk by, she would look up and say "hello." I think I would mumble something in return, but I was still in shock. For at least three days, I felt pretty sorry for myself, then finally, something snapped. *This is* wrong *and not OK! These are lies, I have done nothing wrong.* I got the courage to walk into my BFF's office and say I wanted HR to be part of our conversation with the director.

BFF Viper: "Oh, no need to involve them just yet. Let's just talk to the director." *(MASSIVE RED FLAG. In most states, HR must be at the* table *if an employee asks for* it. *The state I lived in was one of those, and this is definitely something a people manager* with *20+ years of experience like my BFF should have known.)*

I started getting suspicious, so I did my own investigation. I asked my friends in security to pull the security footage of me walking into work every day; I asked for a random sampling of photos from the past six months. I had over 100 photos of me coming and going in a business suit, heels, pantyhose, pearls EVERY SINGLE DAY. By any reasonable standard, I could not be deemed unprofessional or inappropriately dressed. I asked random individuals I would pass by each day if they felt how I dressed was in any way inappropriate. Every single person said I was one of the most professional dressers they had ever worked with.

Finally, the day arrived when I would be vindicated, when the director would tell my BFF how out of line she was, how unprofessional, how disrespectful, etc. I just knew he would lay into her! I was so hurt by what my BFF had done that I didn't really know what my endgame was; I just wanted her to be told she was WAY off base. I wanted the director to pick sides and tell her that she was awful for making me feel like crap, for making me feel dirty, for making me feel wrong, whatever the right words are to describe what she did to me. She was my friend. How could she do this to me? I was screaming inside. Even writing about this experience nearly fifteen years later, I still get emotional about it; betrayal runs deep.

ANOTHER MAJOR RED FLAG ALERT: My BFF and the director walked into the meeting TOGETHER, laughing. I am seated at the table with my 100 pictures of security footage. My BFF proceeded to tell our director why we were there: several individuals approached her, stating that I make them uncomfortable with how I dress. Our director nods his head, never once looking at me.

BFF: "Andrea, do you have anything to say?"

Me: (Internal thoughts) *Why, you backstabbing, horrible human being, I sure do…*

Me: (Real words to the director) "I find this conversation completely unprofessional and unacceptable. I feel personally attacked, and if these complaints were actually made [insert BFF huffing], my manager had a duty to engage HR. Furthermore, here are 100 photos of security footage randomly selected from the past six months of me coming and going from work. You will see I am wearing a conservative business suit every day. Can you please tell me in which photos I am inappropriately dressed?"

In my head, I heard a drum roll and a mic drop. I knew the director would see what was really going on. He would see that my BFF—obviously, out of a fit of jealousy—was lying and personally attacking my credibility. My BFF should be shunned and sent to work in the basement!

Sadly, this is what really occurred...

Our director thumbed through the pictures, paused, and without ever looking at me, said, "Andrea, actually, you make me uncomfortable with how you dress."

It was like I had just been punched in the gut and couldn't breathe. I was floored. It took everything in my power to not burst into tears.

I was devastated.

I gathered the courage to get up and thank them both for their time. Even though it was just three in the afternoon, I went into my office, grabbed my briefcase, to walk to the bus station. My assistant saw my face and asked if I wasokay. I couldn't even muster up the words to say anything to her. I was on the edge of tears and just had to get away. I got a seat in the very back of the bus, put my headphones in, and started blasting the Cranberries' "Zombie" (my go to when I am feeling sad/anger/rage). For the second time in a month, I spent the entire three-hour bus ride home bawling my eyes out.

Even now, it is hard to convey the totality of the emotions I experienced in that one-week period—the betrayal by a friend, the loss of a friend, and the lack of leadership and professionalism from a director I had respected and even admired. My job had become an unbearable situation, and I saw no solution regarding how I could repair my working relationships. I called a good friend with the City and County of San Francisco and asked if he had any openings; he did. Even though it was a step down in both rank and pay, I saw it as a great opportunity to get myself out of hell.

The day after the "conversation" with my BFF and director, I sent a one-paragraph email to both of them.

Me: "I appreciate you taking the time to speak with me yesterday. I am deeply hurt about the baseless accusation you made about my professionalism. I am tending my resignation. I can stay for a month but let me know if you would like me to leave sooner."

Just like that, my six-year career was over. A career I had commuted three hours one way for five days a week for six years was over. I walked away never to speak a word to my BFF or the director again.

# Older Andrea Insert

In hindsight and reflecting on my decision to walk away (even though as you continue to read my story, you will know it ended up being excellent move), it was immature and rash. My reaction was, obviously, understandable, given my level of hurt and betrayal. My BFF and director had at least twenty years of experience on me, and they treated me with no respect. What they did to me was wrong, and I was right to stand up for myself. If I had gone to HR or a member of senior leadership, I believe there would have been a different ending; my situation would have been heard, and my BFF dealt with accordingly. After I left, I found out I was not the first "up and comer" she had done this to, and unfortunately, because I left without even giving an exit interview, she did the same thing to the next person who filled my role.

I let my emotions blind me, and there were people and processes in place to help me through a difficult situation and even manage my emotions better. This experience taught me a tough lesson. The workplace is not the place to have a BFF. It's good to be friendly, kind, and nice to others, but you are all there to do a job and must always stay attuned to the motivations of others. Sadly, everyone you meet on your journey will not want you to be successful, BUT do not let them interfere with your success. Take in all the feedback you receive, good and bad, and truly reflect on it. If the feedback is something that you agree with and want to work on, then do that. If not, stand up for yourself in a professional, diplomatic way, get support from the legal/HR structure your workplace offers, AND document everything. You might not get the support or help you need, but you never know who down the road you might help.

# Kiss My A** Widely Inappropriate Drunken Black Forest Cake

**Ingredients**

**Cakes**

- 2 cups all-purpose flour
- 2 cups white sugar
- 3/4 unsweetened cocoa powder
- 1 1/2 teaspoons baking powder
- ¾ teaspoon baking soda
- 1/2 teaspoon salt
- 3 eggs
- 1 cup milk
- 1/2 cup butter (melted)
- 1 tablespoon vanilla

**Fruit Filling**

- 2 (20 ounce) cans pitted sour cherries
- 1 cup white sugar
- 1/4 cup cornstarch

- 2 teaspoons sour cherry schnapps or Herring's Cherry liquor

**Whipped Cream Frosting**

- 1-quart heavy whipping cream

Note: *Most people sweeten their whipping cream with either white sugar or confectioner's sugar. I don't feel it's necessary, and it makes the cake too sweet. However, if that is your preference, add a cup to the whipping cream as you whip it up.*

**Directions**

Preheat the oven to 350°F. Grease and flour two 9-inch round cake pans; cover the bottoms with waxed paper. In a large bowl, combine flour, sugar, cocoa, baking powder, baking soda, and salt. Add eggs, milk, butter, and 1 tablespoon vanilla; beat until well blended. Pour the batter into prepared pans. Bake for 35 minutes or until a wooden toothpick inserted in centers comes out clean. Cool layers in the pans on wire racks for about 10 minutes, loosen the edges, flip over, and let the cakes cool directly on the racks.

Drain cherries, reserving ½ cup juice. Combine the reserved juice, cherries, 1 cup sugar, and cornstarch in a 2-quart saucepan. Cook over low heat until thickened, stirring constantly. Stir in schnapps or cherry liquor. Let it cool. Beat whipping cream with an electric mixer at high speed until stiff peaks form. With a long-serrated knife, split each cake layer horizontally in half. To assemble, place one cake layer on a plate. Spread with 1 cup whipped cream; top with? cup cherry topping. Top with a second cake layer; repeat layers of frosting and cherry topping. Top with a third cake layer. Frost the sides and top of the cake. Spoon the remaining cherry topping onto the top of the cake.

# Be a Mentor
# Hold the Door Open

I have presented you with several case studies of the bad individuals I have met throughout my professional career. It is important to note that I have written about experiences I have had as a straight, white woman living in one of the world's richest and freest countries, so I would like to recognize my privilege. I can't imagine how brutal the workplace can be for minorities and LGBTQIA individuals. With privilege comes responsibility. I feel it is my duty to constantly ask, "Is a perspective missing from the 'table'?" If yes, I go out and find it and make sure that person has a seat. Additionally, it's important to acknowledge that the playing field is not even and I have an additionalduty to help give opportunity to those who have been marginalized. Being a mentor is one of the best ways I have found to help support others and helps counteract workplace evil.

By holding the door open for those coming behind you, by being supportive and mentoring the next generation, you can be the counterbalance to what can feel like an open pit of despicable human behavior in the workplace.

Take a moment to ask yourself what you will do when you witness a Cretin, Douchebag, or Viper abusing a colleague of yours. Will you say something? Will you stop the bad behavior?

It is important not to get jaded by the bad behavior you will witness and experience. Keep your eyes open for the good because you will meet many amazing folks throughout your journey. I attest there will be more good than bad, but a situation will always play out by how you interpret it and what you learn from it. Reflect on the bad. Never let a bad experience go to waste. Develop action plans on how you would have liked to have dealt with a situation better and use your action plans as your workbook to help yourself and others grow.

On the next page is a list I put together early on in my career highlighting actions I would not do when I was in charge; this list became the foundation for my core management principles. I reference this list on a quarterly basis to make sure I am on track because I never want anyone to feel like I was made to feel by the Cretins, Douchebags, and Vipers I have met in my career. Take a moment to create your own list.

Another way to keep growing and mentoring others is to find individuals that you admire. Outline why you admire them so you can emulate their behaviors and attributes in the workplace.

I have benefited enormously throughout my career from people seeing something in me when I didn't or picking me up in my darkest moments. Later, I share with you three of the most outstanding individuals I have had the honor of meeting and working with during my career. They were mentors, friends, and in some cases, my savior.

*Take a moment to list your mentors and what you admire about them.*

# Your Core Principles

Early in my career, after a series of terrible managers, I wrote down the following list of items I would not do when I was in charge. To this day, I reference this list on a quarterly basis to ensure I am holding myself accountable to the principles I felt were so important as a younger professional.

Through the years, I have done well keeping to my "younger Andrea" principles. The hardest one for me is #5. Though, I firmly believe you shouldn't keep someone in a role just because they have been there a long time; however, that doesn't take away from the fact that it is hard to tell someone to their face that they need to change how they have done their job for years or they will lose it.

#4 is by far the most important on the list. If something is the right thing to do, it's the right thing to do; everything else is just noise.

1. I will never take credit for anyone else's work
2. I will not let bureaucracy be a security blanket or an excuse to not get something accomplished
3. I will not make false promises
4. I will act with integrity
5. I will not promote or keep someone around just because they are a long-term employee
6. I will not become complacent

7. I will treat everyone with respect
8. I will realize when it is time to move on.

What is your list? What will you hold yourself accountable for when you are in charge?

# Your Monthly Mantra

Every month, pull out your personal assessment and ask yourself the following questions:

- Am I getting what I need from my job?
- Am I getting what I want from my job?
- If not,

  o Have I vocalized this to my boss?
  o If yes, what did they say?
  o If not, do I accept this?

- What are my next steps?
- Am I following my personal assessment? If no, why not? Should I change it?
- Did I mentor anyone this past month?

# The Mentors

*The following three individuals' have been influential to not only my career, but also my life. I am a better person, because I had the opportunity to meet and work with them. I have designed a special tribute recipe, centered around the attributes I most admire about each of the mentors*

## The OG EM: Ms. Avagene Moore

In November 2007, I attended my first International Association of Emergency Managers (IAEM) conference in Reno, Nevada. I was still pretty junior in my career, and I felt it was a good way for me to network and grow in the field. Additionally, I needed to escape. I was dealing with the most devastating personal decision I had made so far in my life; I sent my teenage son away to a reform school in Utah on October 31, 2007.

His behavior had turned my homelife into a war zone putting a serious strain on my marriage and I was commuting three hours one way to work each day. To say that my life was stressful would have been an understatement. I did not have the capacity or ability to deal with the situation, so I felt my only solution was to send him away. I did not share what I was going through with anyone not even with my closest friends. There is not a day since October 31, 2007, that I have not wished I just reached out for guidance or help. At the time, I was working in a law enforcement environment as one of the only females and I did not feel I could share what was going on. Especially since it was personal not work related and I was very much a "check your sh\*\*" at the door kind of person. I naively thought I could separate my personal life from my work life, but my son grounded me, and since I had him young, we matured together. With him gone, I was in a freefall.

I remember having all this personal trauma replaying in my mind as I stepped into the conference hall and immediately became overwhelmed. I felt the sinking feeling of a panic attack coming on. With my heart pounding and gasping for air, I turned around trying to find the exit door. I remember clutching the conference bag close to my chest almost like a security blanket and hearing my internal voice saying, "Please do not start crying. Please do not start crying."

Somehow, Ms. Avagene must have sensed I needed help. As I was walking out, she walked right up to me and said in the most elegant Southern drawl you can imagine, "Are you ok?" "You seem very upset." "I do not believe I know you, but I want to. My name is Avagene Moore. There are not that many of us girls here, so we must stick together."

I was taken off guard. I did not know what to do, and I think I just stared at her for way too long mindlessly blinking. Finally, all I could muster up was a faint, "No, I am notokay." Ms. Avagene took my arm and led to me into an empty conference room. She gave me a hug, pulled up a chair and said "honey, tell me what is going on. You will feel better.

I sobbed for ten minutes straight telling Ms. Avagene everything. She just let me talk and cry everything out, holding my hand, listening. She was right I did feel better, much better. She asked if I still wanted to leave or if she could be my host to show me around. I decided to stay.

Ms. Avagene escorted me back to the main conference hall and regaled me with stories of past conferences. I remember thinking how perfect she was. I wanted to be just like her; she exuded confidence. Her blond hair was beautifully done in an updo, and she was dressed in an impeccable suit with pearls on. I loved that she was unabashedly feminine, especially since pretty much the dress code for an emergency manager is a polo, khaki pants, a clipboard, and a tactical belt and vest (which, BTW, looks HORRIBLE on a large-busted woman like yours truly.}

I wanted to emulate her in every way.

I would come to learn Ms. Avagene was one of the first female presidents of the International Association of Emergency Managers, and I quickly became her Number One fan girl. That day, Ms. Avagene even convinced me to do a video message in support of IAEM and why attending the conference was so important.

As time came and went and my career changed several times, I did not get a lot of opportunities to speak to Ms. Avagene, but I could always count on running into her at the annual conference. I could always feel her before I saw her; she was one of those people who was effervescent and larger than life. She was always up to something: leading a tour for students, introducing someone, and so on. Her grace and capacity to support others seemed limitless.

In early 2020 when I took the opportunity to lead Walmart's Emergency Management Department, I leaned heavily on the lesson I had learned from Ms. Avagene. Ms. Avagene taught me how important it is to actively check on others. As a people leader in charge of the world's largest retailer responding to a global pandemic, I had a duty to ensure my team was taken care of both physically and mentally. The push to virtual tore down any perceived boundaries between personal and work lives; increasing an already heightened stress load for everyone. Everyone was impacted by the pandemic but in very different ways, many struggling with personal and family issues. I remembered years ago how horrible it felt to be going through a traumatic experience where I was all alone. I also remembered how the three simple words that Ms. Avagene asked me- Are You Ok-, changed my life and helped me see a path forward. I wanted to do the same for my team by creating a culture of checking in on each other. Asking if someone is okay and not taking a "fine" for an answer. I was open with my team and shared what I was dealing with which made them comfortable with sharing how they were feeling. Being vulnerable created an environment where it was okay to say you were struggling because you knew you had a team that had your back. Even though I spent the majority of my tenure with Walmart working virtually, I felt so close to my team because of the safe space we had created.

There was so much that happened in 2020 that was devastating, but the news of Ms. Avagene's passing on Christmas Eve 2020 hit me the hardest. She had no idea how she saved me back in 2007. It is because of Ms. Avagene that mentorship is so important to me. To this day, I can still hear her encouraging me, and I hope to be that voice for many others and to carry on her legacy.

Thank you, Ms. Avagene.

# Ms. Avagene's Grace and Style Southern Tea Cakes

### Ingredients

- 4 cups all-purpose flour
- 1 teaspoon baking soda
- 2 teaspoons baking powder
- 2 cups sugar
- 2 eggs
- ½ cup buttermilk
- 1 cup unsalted butter, softened
- A splash of your favorite Tennessee whiskey *(it's only Jack Daniels for me!)*

### Directions

Preheat the oven to 350° F. Sift the flour, baking soda, and baking powder together into a large bowl. Add all remaining ingredients and mix well. The dough will be a bit sticky. On a floured surface shape, put the dough into a disk, cover with plastic wrap, and refrigerate for at least an hour. Flour the surface again and roll the dough out until approximately an inch thick. Using your favorite cookie cutters, cut the dough and bake for about 10 minutes. The edges of the cookies will be a nice golden brown.

# The Unflappable Mr. Threat

## Threatisms

- "Is there a grenade on the floor? If not, go out of my office and come back in."
- "Be careful which doors you decide to kick in; they might just swing back and hit you."
- "It is better to learn how to take a punch, then throw one."

## Background

I joined FEMA's Louisiana Recovery Office in May 2010—a week after the historic Deepwater Horizon oil spill, which nearly wiped out a third of the US fishing industry. It was five years post-Hurricane Katrina, there was a new presidential administration in office, and even though the Saints had won the Super Bowl, recovery was sluggish for the entire State of Louisiana. After interviewing for 12 different positions *(yes, 12, I was very determined* to *work for FEMA),* I was finally selected to serve as the external affairs director, the person in charge of telling the story of the recovery effort. I was so excited to get the opportunity. I really didn't give much thought to how challenging my new job was going to be and how ill prepared I was for it.

I still remember arriving at my small apartment in the French Quarter. New Orleans had everything to me—the best food, the best music, the most dynamic people. And even though the city had suffered one of the most devasting natural disasters in US history, the feeling of strength and resiliency was everywhere. It was that feeling, that culture of resiliency I wanted to tap into, to help showcase the rebuilding efforts going on.

I had a lot of heart but was very inexperienced and naive to notice or deal with the hot mess of politics I had walked into. I was very thankful my new boss noticed my heart and intention and took me under his wing *(within one week of being at the office, everyone* started calling *me Frisco Red; my optimism and spirit was* not being *perceived well).* My boss was a gentleman by the name of Joe Threat. Mr. Threat was a career marine before his role at FEMA; he fought in Vietnam and was awarded the Purple Heart. He has been a great coach and mentor to me and is truly one of the greatest men I have had the opportunity to work for, and now I get to call him my friend.

Mr. Threat had been personally impacted by Hurricane Katrina, losing his home, as well as several of his other family members losing theirs. Mr. Threat didn't need to step into the Louisiana Recovery Office and take over as the executive director, but he wanted to help his community.

It is no secret that the response to Hurricane Katrina and the initial recovery efforts were abysmal and lacking in a strategy to support those impacted. There were many failings, but to me, the most notable was the lack of engagement with the impacted community on how they wanted to rebuild and recover. When I arrived, I couldn't believe the lack of the local voice and how it appeared politics and outdated laws were dictating what was rebuilt, who received money, and even how debris was removed *(yes, even at year five,* there were *massive* amounts of *abandoned properties* throughout New *Orleans}.* It was heartbreaking to see, and this approach to recovery was completely ineffective and demoralizing. Just think if you were a small child and every day you had to walk to school past abandoned properties that had brown-stained water lines showing how high the flood waters rose or search and rescue tags, indicating how many people had died in that house.

If you are constantly reminded of your worst day, day after day, you can never recover.

I wanted so badly to fix this and help. I remember walking into Mr. Threat's office and asking him what he thought about doing a complete 180 on our approach to reaching out to local communities: "Why don't we ask the community how they would like to rebuild?" Mr. Threat said yes, and my team and I embarked on a massive outreach campaign regarding FEMA's recovery efforts. This consisted of one-on-one meetings with mayors, legislatures, local leaders, and the media, in addition to the development of several publications documenting recovery efforts and the establishment of a significant social media and web presence. I am immensely proud of what Mr. Threat, my team, and I were able to accomplish. Our approach helped to completely transform the public's perception of FEMA, culminating with FEMA's participation in over 300 ground breaking, ribbon-cutting ceremonies, the local media coining a new acronym,

"TGFF" (Thank God for FEMA); and the mayor of New Orleans at the time, Mitch Landrieu, stating FEMA was his "best friend" in the Katrina recover. This was one of my proudest professional accomplishments.

## *Continued from the Cretin page 24*

I called Mr. Threat balling. I asked him to let me come back to the recovery office. I told him what had happened. How I had humiliated myself, crying like an absolute hysterical baby. Mr. Threat didn't say anything. I literally started begging him to let me come home. I figured at this point I had no shame and nothing left of my dignity.

Mr. Threat calmly said, "No. Andrea, you need to listen to me. You are not going to be judged by what just happened. You are going to be judged by how you come back from it."

I was livid with him. "So the answer is no? I have to stay here?" I just hung up on him. I was so upset. I went back to my office and bailed for what seemed like an hour and was trying to figure out if I could just quit.

While feeling very sorry for myself, I got a call from FEMA headquarters that Homeland Security Secretary Napolitano needed a briefing on the flooding situation in the next couple of hours because she was briefing the President, at 5 a.m. I was so beside myself, I had totally lost track of time. I was still sick to my stomach for what had happened to me and SO mad at Mr. Threat, but this task helped refocus me. I honestly believed the work my team and I were doing to support the flooding response was good and helpful, even though my leadership obviously didn't support or protect me. I was terrified that I would run into the Cretin, so I slinked around and gathered my team to prepare the briefing. I remember we got the briefing to the Secretary's office around 1 a.m. I told the team to get some sleep and that I would hang around to see if any changes were needed. Knowing the FCO still had his 0600 meeting, and I would receive zero consideration for working all night, I just camped in my office overnight, locked the door, and slept under the desk. I think I slept for about five minutes. I remember walking like a zombie to the FCO's meeting. I am sure I smelled because I hadn't showered in a few days, but I honestly didn't care.

I arrived at the meeting about five minutes early and sat near the front; the Cretin always sat in the back, blocking the door, but somehow, I beat him there. The FCO walked in as the other members of his leadership team filed in.

The FCO stated, "Before we get started, I have an announcement to make. I received a call early today from Secretary Napolitano's office. Ms. Davis, she was very impressed with the briefing you and your team compiled, especially given the short turnaround time you had. I commend you for your work." He stood up and all his leadership stood up and gave me a standing ovation, EVEN the Cretin! I think I was so exhausted both mentally and physically that I don't really remember how I responded. I probably just smiled and nodded but really don't have a clue. The meeting ended, and I gathered my things. I wanted to walk to the other side of the building to tell my team the good news. I took a shortcut through the parking lot. I stopped dead in my tracks as I saw Mr. Threat drive up, get out of his car, head straight to the Cretin, and calmly but firmly tell the Cretin if he ever treated a member of his staff the way he treated me, he would make sure he was fired. He got back in his car and drove back to New Orleans. (It's a 90-mile drive from New Orleans to Baton Rouge.)

Mr. Threat didn't know that I saw him that day nor what he had done. What he did shows you how great he is. His advice to me was spot on; I had to find the strength in myself to handle the Cretin and not let his bad behavior impact me. However, Mr. Threat knew what the Cretin was doing was wrong and that he did need to be handled. He handled him with no fanfare or ever saying anything about it. The Cretin never bothered me again. In fact, his government career ended up being pretty short-lived.

# Mr. Threat's Calm, Cool, and Collected Take-No-Crap Peach Cobbler

Ingredients

- 1/2 cup unsalted butter, melted
- 1 cup all—purpose flour
- 1 1/2 cup sugar, divided
- 1 tablespoon baking power
- ¼ teaspoon salt
- 1 cup half and half
- ½ cup light brown sugar
- ¼ cups fresh peach slices (if it's off-season, thawed frozen peaches are a good substitute}
- 1 tablespoon lemon juice
- Sprinkle of nutmeg
- Your favorite cinnamon (trust me!) or vanilla ice cream

Directions

Preheat the oven to 375° F. Drizzle melted butter into a blarge baking dish. Combine flour, 1 cup sugar, baking powder, and salt; add half and half, stirring just until dry ingredients are moistened. Set aside. Bring the remaining in

½ cup sugar, ½ cup light brown sugar, peach slices, and lemon juice to a boil over high heat, stirring constantly; pour in baking dish. Drop large spoonfuls of the flour mixture over the peaches. Sprinkle with nutmeg. Bake at 375° F for 40—45 minutes, or until golden brown. Serve the cobbler warm, with ice cream.

# Dr. Jones

In 1994, my son was a feisty three-year-old, and I was studying for my paralegal certificate at the local junior college and working three different waitressing jobs, one with graveyard shifts. I am sure, to an outsider looking at my situation, my son and I must have looked pretty dire; however, to me, I had all my goals aligned and felt I was taking good care of my son. He was a happy, healthy little boy, who sometimes got to go to class with me, or sleep in one of the booths at the restaurant. It was a great adventure!

Reflecting on the early 90s, they always feel like such a blur, and I believe that is because I don't really recall sleeping very much. Even when you are young, a lack of sleep can lead to an almost zombie state of existence. Waiting tables for the graveyard shift almost always felt like an alternate reality. The grave "regulars" were always an interesting mix of students, insomniacs, cops, and just plain weirdos. There was even a group of elderly men who felt death was knocking and believed if they stayed up drinking twenty-cent coffee and playing cards in a diner booth until 3 a.m. every night, they would somehow cheat death. It was an interesting existence for sure.

All my regulars knew I was a single teen mom working and going to school. Most were always very generous with advice and tips and even helped with my homework. Working graveyard shifts, 3 a.m. was the best time to get homework done. The drunks would have had their last meal, and the next rush wouldn't start until around 5 a.m., as the cops were heading into their 6 a.m. shifts.

One early morning, in January 1994, I turned on the morning news at the restaurant. Back in the early 90s, there were pretty much three main networks, and all three were playing the same story. A large devastating earthquake had struck Southern California in Northridge. The regulars asked me to turn up the volume, and I remember standing there glued to the screen while holding a coffee pot, watching the horrifying pictures of downed bridges and out-of-control fires. The footage was interrupted by the newscaster saying the leading seismologist, Dr. Jones from the USGS, would be holding a press conference shortly to brief on the situation. I filled up everyone's coffee cups so I could get back to the briefing. I had never heard the term seismologist before, let alone known there was a science dedicated to earthquakes. My interest was further piqued due to the name—Dr. Jones. I know this is lame, but I was a huge Indiana Jones/Harrison Ford fan, so visions of him were in my mind. I couldn't wait to see what he looked like! The press conference started, and my jaw dropped. Dr. Jones was definitely not Harrison Ford. Dr. Jones was a female! AND she took the press conference while holding her young son who had fallen asleep. A female, MOM, scientist briefing the media? My mind was blown.

The image of Dr. Jones holding a press conference with her young son is still etched in my brain. To me, that image validated I wasn't nuts to think I could go to law school, be a mom, and put food on the table. Yes, uncommon, but very possible, especially after what I had just witnessed. I had an immediate boost of confidence and renewed belief I was going to make it.

Over twenty years would pass before my career path would cross that of Dr. Jones. I had the honor of hosting her retirement party from the USGS and got to tell her firsthand the impact she made on my life so many years prior. That day in 1994, Dr. Jones was just being herself, doing what she needed to do, and didn't care what the world thought. She gave me the confidence to do the same.

# Dr. Jones's Self-Confident, Own Who You Are Hot Fudge Brownie Sundae

**Ingredients**

**Brownies**

- ½ cup unsalted butter, melted
- 2 tablespoons water
- 1 cup milk chocolate chips
- 2 cups semisweet chocolate chips
- 2 tablespoon Bailey's Irish Cream OR vanilla
- 2 large eggs
- ¾ cup all—purpose flour
- 1 cup granulated sugar
- ½ cup powdered sugar
- ½ teaspoon salt
- Cooking spray

**Hot Fudge Sauce**

- 1 ½ cups granulated sugar
- 1 bag dark chocolate chips
- 1 cup heavy whipping cream

- ½ cup butter
- 2 teaspoons vanilla extract
- Pinch of salt
- Your favorite ice cream (a simple vanilla is best)

## Directions

In a large pan, melt butter, chocolate chips, and water on low heat. Stir slowly until mixed and melted. Remove from heat. In the same pan, add Bailey's Irish Cream and eggs. Mix in flour, sugars, and salt. Spray an 8 x 8-inch glass baking dish with cooking spray. Bake for 40—45 minutes, stick a toothpick in the middle; if it comes out clean, your brownies are done. Let cool in a pan for about 10 minutes. Make hot fudge sauce. In a medium saucepan, mix sugar, chocolate chips, and whipping cream. Bring to a boil. Add butter, vanilla, and salt. Stir constantly until the sauce thickens (about 3—5 minutes). Remove from heat. Cut your favorite piece of brownie, add a dollop of ice cream, and drizzle the hot fudge sauce on top.

# Rednado Goes into The Great Unknown

I often get asked why I left my job with the Walt Disney Company, a job I publicly stated several times was my dream job. I even said I felt like I had won the job lottery, because it never felt like I was working, and it truly was an opportunity of a lifetime. I was working in the emergency management field for a company that made a business of selling good feelings. For five and half of my seven years with the conpany, it truly was an awesome experience. My team and I got to create preparedness programming for the enterprise and travel the globe; I had the amazing opportunity to travel to 49 different countries, before I left. Everyday seemed like an adventure, one which I got to experience with some of my best friends. It was at Disney I was given one of my favorite and most fitting nicknames—Rednado. My assistant coined the nickname after I slammed into my locked office door, late for a meeting, and ended up flying/falling into her cubicle. That was the first of many times we would laugh hysterically for a good two minutes. When I reflect on my time at Disney, for the most part, I can remember the constant sound of laughter and the feeling of happiness.

Unfortunately, that feeling came to a screeching halt after I was continuously harassed, demeaned and repeatedly disrespected by a Cretin. This Cretin decided to change the entire crisis response structure of the company and train on it without even discussing it with me or my team. He unilaterally decided his region was too "unique" to adhere to company and international emergency management standards. My favorite complaint of his was when he proclaimed the international *Great Shake-Out* earthquake drill (which Dr. Jones was instrumental in creating) was not relevant to his region. Mind you, his region had suffered from some of the greatest, most damaging earthquakes in all of history. His behavior was not only damaging to my program's reputation, but also putting the company at risk.

I stood up for myself and my program; I expected my leadership to do the same. Even though they had a legal obligation (and I would argue a moral and ethical one) to support me and ensure I was protected from such bad behavior, they chose to do the opposite. I went to my boss, he did nothing. I went to the Cretin's boss, he did nothing. I went to the head of the division, he did nothing. I went to HR, they did nothing. Worse, when I went to HR, I was deemed a traitor, and my leadership started attacking me professionally and gaslighting me. I was directly told by my boss in a staff meeting in front of colleagues that "I was too smart to think I was being harassed." The division head said, in writing, my response to the Cretin was "too harsh". To add to the injustice, I took direct, documented evidence of my harasser's activities to HR, and nothing was done.

Prior to joining Disney, there were always rumors of the "good old boys club," but I was so enamored by the brand I didn't pay attention to them. I let a lot of things slide, and to be honest, I didn't want to believe them. However, having it happen directly to me, I couldn't hide my head in the sand anymore. Sadly, I did everything right about reporting what happened to me and followed all the right steps, but no actions were taken to stop the harassment. When I got wind that the Cretin was to be promoted, my heart broke. Putting aside his deplorable behavior; my scope, experience, and tenure with the company was much greater than his, so it made no sense that he was being promoted, other than the obvious: he had a penis, and I didn't.

Seeing no hope in sight that I would be helped or even heard, I called a good friend and asked if he thought I would be a good fit for a job that he was leaving for a new opportunity. He put my resume in front of the head of the department who liked me and offered me the job.

It was a heartbreaking decision to leave a job I loved, people I treasured, and the city I was born in to embark on a brand new journey and start over. For the second time in my career, I jumped into the unknown.

On January 4, 2020, I got on a plane, devastated, to Bentonville, Arkansas, with two suitcases and my cat, Mr. Boo. I took an opportunity with the world's largest company—Walmart—as their head of Global Emergency Management. My first day on the job was January 6, 2020.

Of course, I had no idea, like the rest of the world, how my life was about to change and what was in store for me...

And to top it off, my cookbooks, which I had been collecting since I was 18, somehow didn't make it into the moving truck and were forever lost.

# Rednado's Broken-Hearted Frozen Lemon Tart

Ingredients

- 1/2 cup unsalted butter, melted
- Half a bag of graham crackers, smashed into bits (best to place them into a Ziploc bag and smash with a spoon)
- 1 cup of heavy whipping cream
- 1/2 can sweetened condensed milk
- 1/2 cup of freshly squeezed lemon juice
- 1 teaspoon grated lemon rind

Directions

Mix melted butter and crushed graham crackers in a bowl. Press buttered crumbs into a pie plate using the back of a spoon. Place in the refrigerator for about 10 minutes. Using a mixer, whip the cream until it is stiff. Slowly add the rest of the ingredients. Fold the ingredients into the prepared pie shell. Place in the freezer for a good three hours; overnight is best. Let it sit a few minutes before serving.

# Self-Acceptance Cherry Pie Recipe

It is definitely hard to stand up for yourself and for others. It's hard to figure out what matters to you, and it's hard to get back up if you have been knocked down more than your fair share. Additionally, if you make a decision that goes against society's "grain" or expectations, your path will not be easy. If you can, I recommend investing time in your decision-making process. I use the first aid method: look at all six sides of the decision—up, down, and all around. Poke holes in your thought process. Ask yourself if you are making the decision based on emotions or logic. What is your "why" behind taking this approach over another?

Obviously, sometimes you must make a quick decision with the facts that you have on hand. When you can, reflect on it, and if it was the wrong call, say that and own it. You will make mistakes, but don't make them worse by digging your heels in just to "stay right." The best leaders I have worked for were not perfect people. They made bad calls, but what set them apart from everyone else was their ability to reflect and say I made a mistake. That's the kind of leader I strive to be. There are times I feel like I am doing great, and then there are days when I let my emotions get the better of me and really suck. But it is important to not get stuck or feel sorry for yourself; that serves no one, especially you.

Find your coping mechanism. Baking helped me through so many tough times. What has helped you? If you make a call to be all in on something, there is a chance you might stand alone. Be ready for that. Don't expect people to agree with, stand by, or even support your decision. After all, it was you who made the decision; they did not. Find a hobby or habit that will keep you grounded as you go through your professional journey.

My journey so far has had a lot of learnings, both good and bad, but I think my biggest learning is that with every experience, both positive and negative, you must decide what you want to take from it. I think back to my first experience with a Queen Bee Viper who told me, "You are just not management material." What would have happened if I had listened to her? I might not have applied for a management job if the voice inside of me hadn't said, "No, you are wrong, and I will prove it." Even though I didn't immediately get selected for a management position, applying for a management role forced me to see that where I was currently at was not the right place for me. I started looking into another management position in emergency operations, which opened a door to a career of a lifetime.

What if I hadn't listened to Mr. Threat and found the strength to go back and work around the Cretin?

Truly reflect on the negative comments you receive throughout your career. Ask yourself, is there any validity to them? If yes, what aspects do you want to work on? If no, write the comment down, and next to it, write "This is not true. This comment was made out of fear, jealousy, or just plain bias. I do not accept it." Consciously decide to move on from it.

Finally, accept the fact that you will make mistakes along the way, but don't miss the opportunity to learn and grow from them. And when you need an extra special pick me up, make yourself some delicious Self-Acceptance Cherry Pie. You deserve it!

# Self-Acceptance Cherry Pie

## Ingredients

### Filling

- 1 1/4 cups sugar
- 3 tablespoons cornstarch
- ¼ teaspoon salt
- 1 tablespoon butter, softened
- 2 cans pitted tart cherries, drained: reserve / cup juice
- ¼ teaspoon almond extract
- Splash of brandy
- Two squeezes of a fresh lemon

### Crust

*Remember the name of this recipe is Self-Acceptance Cherry Pie, so it is okay to just buy a crust from the store. Pie crust tends to be the bane of my existence. For some reason, my crusts are always too crumbly or lumpy. Allow yourself to sometimes to just cut your losses!*

- 2 ½ cups all-purpose flour
- 1 tablespoon granulated sugar

- ½ teaspoon salt
- 1 cup frozen unsalted butter, grated
- 2 tablespoons orange juice
- 2—4 tablespoons ice water

**Directions**

Preheat the oven to 400° F. For pie crusts, mix flour, sugar, salt, and sugar in a bowl. Grate butter into the bowl; slowly mix (by hand or with a pastry blender if you have one). Add water and orange juice one tablespoon at a time. Mix with your hands. If the dough is too crumbly, add another tablespoon, but pie crusts do best with less handling. Divide the dough in half to create two disks. Wrap the disks separately in plastic; refrigerate for at least an hour. As the pie crusts cool, drain cherries, reserving in cup juice, in a medium bowl. Combine sugar, cornstarch, and salt. In a separate bowl, combine cherry juice, almond extract, a splash of brandy, and lemon squeezes, and add to the dry ingredients, mixing well. Add cherries and mix well again. Add butter. Remove the dough from the refrigerator and roll it on a floured surface into a 14-inch round. Carefully, move the rolled dough into the pie pan. Make sure the dough goes over the edge of the pie dish; using a fork, create a decorative border. Pour the pie filling into the pie crust. Roll the second disk, cut into pieces, and create a fun design on top of the pie. If you have any dough left over, using your favorite cookie cutter, cut a piece and place the dough in the middle of the pie. Bake for 50— minutes. Your pie should be nice and bubbly and the crust a nice golden brown by the time you pull it out.

CPSIA information can be obtained
at www.ICGtesting.com
Printed in the USA
BVHW051024110723
667064BV00013B/1144